The EVERYTHING KIDS' MORE PUZZLES BOOK

From mazes to hidden pictures—
and hours of fun in between!

SCOT RITCHIE

A adamsmedia

Avon, Massachusetts

PUBLISHER Karen Cooper

DIRECTOR OF ACQUISITIONS AND INNOVATION Paula Munier

MANAGING EDITOR, EVERYTHING® SERIES Lisa Laing

COPY CHIEF Casey Ebert

ACQUISITIONS EDITOR Katrina Schroeder

ASSOCIATE DEVELOPMENT EDITOR Hillary Thompson

EDITORIAL ASSISTANT Ross Weisman

EVERYTHING® SERIES COVER DESIGNER Erin Alexander

LAYOUT DESIGNERS Colleen Cunningham, Elisabeth Lariviere, Ashley Vierra, Denise Wallace

An Everything® Series Book.
Everything® and everything.com® are registered trademarks of F+W Media, Inc.

Published by Adams Media, a division of F+W Media, Inc.
57 Littlefield Street, Avon, MA 02322. U.S.A.
www.adamsmedia.com

ISBN 10: 1-4405-0647-7
ISBN 13: 978-1-4405-0647-5
eISBN 10: 1-4405-0648-5
eISBN 13: 978-1-4405-0648-2

Printed by RR Donnelley, Harrisonburg, VA, U.S.

10 9 8 7 6 5 4 3 2 1

August 2010

This publication is designed to provide accurate and authoritative information with regard to the subject matter covered. It is sold with the understanding that the publisher is not engaged in rendering legal, accounting, or other professional advice. If legal advice or other expert assistance is required, the services of a competent professional person should be sought.
—From a *Declaration of Principles* jointly adopted by a Committee of the American Bar Association and a Committee of Publishers and Associations

Many of the designations used by manufacturers and sellers to distinguish their products are claimed as trademarks. When those designations appear in this book and Adams Media was aware of a trademark claim, the designations have been printed with initial capital letters.

Interior illustrations and puzzles by Scot Ritchie.

This book is available at quantity discounts for bulk purchases.
For information, please call 1-800-289-0963.

Visit the entire Everything® series at www.everything.com

CONTENTS

INTRODUCTION

If you find yourself laughing out loud and being challenged, perplexed, and stumped, then we're doing our job with the latest puzzle book from Adams Media, *The Everything® Kids' More Puzzles Book*.

In the dictionary, you'll find that the word "puzzle" is defined as "a test of cleverness or a toy that exercises your mind." We like that definition because it describes what we set out to do in the newest *The Everything® Kids' More Puzzles Book*. We're sure you'll enjoy the challenge and fun of the 100 puzzles you'll find inside. Adding to the enjoyment is lots of interesting information, sprinkled in among the games. You will be learning without even knowing it! Check out Chapter 10; did you know that out of the 40,000 species of spider known to man, only 1 is vegetarian?

This is a great book to take on a road trip or family vacation or even to keep you company in the smallest room in the house! With connect-the-dots games, mazes, and spelling quizzes, you'll be entertained for hours.

As an added bonus, keep your eyes open for Max, our puzzle-loving cat who makes himself at home wandering onto puzzle pages. Sometimes he's seeing what's going on; other times he just wants to curl up and take a nap. See if you can spot how many times he shows up in the book. But make sure it's Max, because there are other felines sprinkled through the book as well! You'll know Max by the 3 stripes on his tail.

To get you started, here's a memory puzzle you can do with your eyes closed! First, look at the scene for 5 seconds and memorize as much as you can. Now, cover it with your hand and see if you can answer these questions. How many balloons is Max holding? What is on the floor—a baseball or football? What time does the clock say?

Now that you're warmed up, why not turn the page, sharpen your pencil (and your mind), and get puzzling! Enjoy!

Threeosaurus Hideaway

Dr. Smith has just discovered a creepy cave with a collection of weird animals. She knows one of them is the elusive Short-Haired Threeosaurus, but she's having trouble identifying which one is which. Can you help her? The correct Threeosaurus must have:

✔ 3 toes on the front and 3 on the back
✔ A marking on its left hind leg
✔ No band around the neck
✔ 3 marks on its back
✔ Long floppy ears
✔ 2 horns
✔ 3 tails
✔ 1 tooth

NEW TO YOU

Recently, scientists discovered 40 new species of animals in a volcanic crater on the island of New Guinea. They include a frog with fangs, a fish that grunts, and a species of rat believed to be the biggest in the world. These animals have no fear of humans, having never seen us before!

Forgetful Dr. Frankenstein

Dr. Frankenstein is trying to build a monster, but he's so forgetful he can't find all the body parts. Can you find everything hidden in his lab?

- ✘ 2 sets of teeth
- ✘ 2 legs
- ✘ 2 hands
- ✘ 1 ear
- ✘ 2 hearts
- ✘ 2 fingers
- ✘ 5 eyeballs
- ✘ 2 noses

MARY'S MONSTER

Mary Shelley's most famous book, *Frankenstein; or The Modern Prometheus*, was published in 1818 when she was only 21 years old. She started to write it when she was 18.

Monsters are busy at night scaring people, but during the day, they have lots of free time. Gertrude loves scary word games. Can you help her out by seeing how many words you can find below?

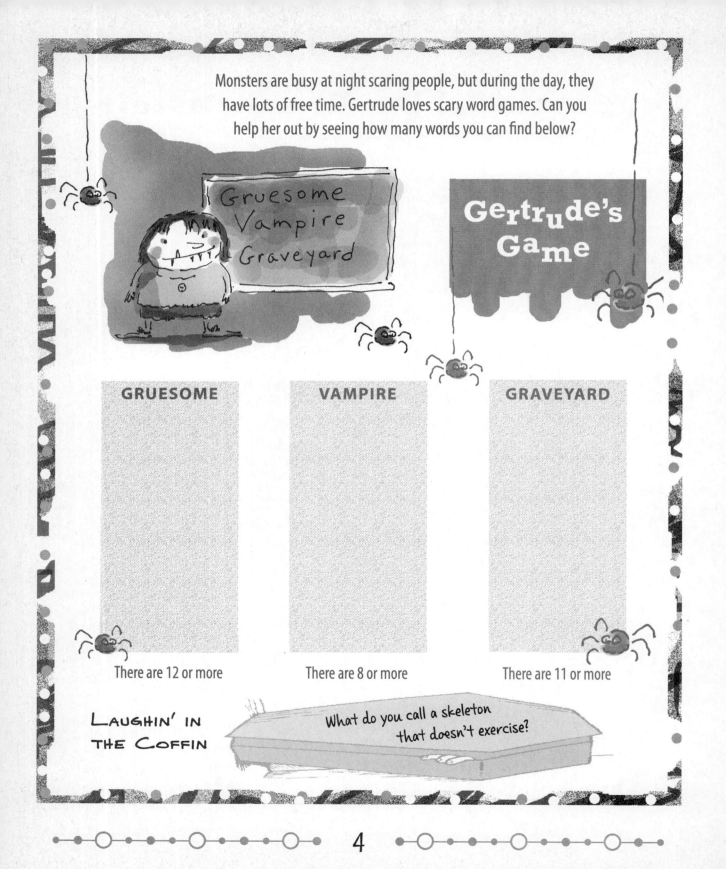

Gruesome
Vampire
Graveyard

Gertrude's Game

GRUESOME

VAMPIRE

GRAVEYARD

There are 12 or more

There are 8 or more

There are 11 or more

LAUGHIN' IN THE COFFIN

What do you call a skeleton that doesn't exercise?

Sp🕸🕸ky Spider

Don't you hate it when a spooky mutant monster spider gets between you and your home? Luckily, Josh knows the route. Can you find it?

All spiders have 8 legs, but only a few have fangs. Is that true or false?

?

start

finish

Stinky Stuff

Can you sniff out these things that go bad or just plain stink?

LDO OKSSC

YTIDR EFET

PRITSAM

LIMK

IHSF

Critter Chaos

Insects have some pretty amazing names. There are actually only 4 bug names here, but the words have been separated. Can you figure out which words go together to make proper names?

FLEA

MIMOSA

MAPLEWORM

PEA

GRAPE

WEBWORM

GREENSTRIPED

WEEVIL

BEETLE

SO SILLY

These bugs are having a fun time. Want to join them? To join in the silly sayings, all you have to do is figure out the first letter.

__urple __arrots __lay __roudly

__low __nakes __lide __outh

__y __other __ixes __onkey __usic

__hildren __arefully __hoose __heese

__ossy __ugs __uild __arricades

There's a big parade today. Everybody has brought along a flag, but one of them doesn't belong. Cross out the one that doesn't fit within each group.

FUNNY FLAGS

A parade is a great place to meet a *vexillologist*. What do you think that is?

HURRY HARBOR

This harbor master is very busy. He has to figure out which ships add up to 40; all the rest he has to turn away. Can you tell which one will get in?

$100 + 1 + 7 - 88 + 14 + 5$

$36 \times 2 - 32$

$5 + 5 + 6 + 10 + 11 + 1 + 3$

$11 \times 7 + 3 - 30 + 10 \times 2$

$60 - 20 - 2$

$9 - 8 + 28 + 10 - 5 + 7$

$2 \times 10 + 25$

MUSSEL MIX UP

This junior naturalist is going to harvest some mussels, but she has to be careful. She can only take the ones that are ready to be eaten. They have 2 stripes and 3 dots on them. How many can you find?

Medieval Mix Up

Something's wrong in this medieval home. Can you find the 10 things that weren't even invented yet?

THE ABOVE-AVERAGE AGES

Even though the Middle Ages (5th to the 15th centuries) were called the Dark Ages, there were actually many great inventions during that time: the printing press, the hourglass, eyeglasses, the mechanical clock, the wheelbarrow, and the spinning wheel.

This looks like a beautiful day, but there is something seriously surreal about the scene. Can you find the 13 things that just aren't right?

REAL SURREAL

The style of painting called Surrealism shows scenes you might see in a dream. The artists hope the unusual images will make viewers look at the world in new and different ways.

Happy Princess

This happy princess has some valuable things she has to remember in case they get stolen. Can you help her? Look at the scene for 1 minute and remember as much as you can. Then, cover it with a piece of paper. Now, see if you can answer the questions below.

1. How many crowns are there?

2. How many shoes are on the floor?

3. What is the title of the book?

4. Does the bedspread have stripes or dots?

5. Is there a cat or a dog on the pillow?

6. What is hanging on the wall?

7. What is on top of the cabinet?

8. What is the princess holding?

AMERICAN ROYALTY

The princess Victoria Ka'iulani was named after her family's close friend, Queen Victoria. Hawaii is the only state in America to have royalty.

Lucky 7

This superstitious dragon is doing his spring cleaning. He does a lot of plundering, but always gets 7 of each thing (because 7 is his lucky number!). It looks like he's in for a surprise. Can you spot the things that don't show up 7 times?

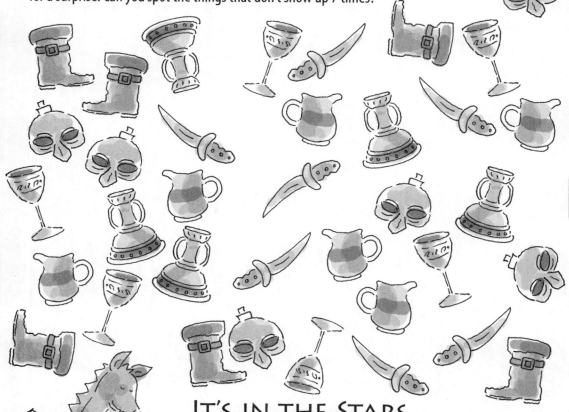

It's in the Stars

One explanation for why 7 is a lucky number is that ancient people could only see what they considered to be 7 planets. They included the Sun, Moon, Mercury, Venus, Mars, Jupiter, and Saturn.

Lonely Dragon

This dragon is lonely, but he's also very picky about who he will play with. Read the statements below and see whom he will choose. His new friend must have:

✦ At least 3 spikes on his head
✦ 1 stripe on his neck or tail
✦ At least 3 spikes on his tail or back
✦ At least 2 teeth
✦ No spots on his body
✦ A head a lighter color than the body

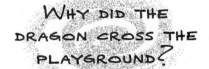

WHY DID THE DRAGON CROSS THE PLAYGROUND?

Dragon Draw

This dragon is pulling a disappearing act. But if you draw quickly, you can keep him visible! His face has to have 2 bulging eyes, 8 BIG sharp teeth, flames coming from his mouth, and 2 pointy ears.

Mythical Mystery

What are we looking at here? He's very shy, so you'll have to break the code to read his greeting.

This prince loves to read, but something has knocked all his books off the shelf. Can you put them back in order? The titles all have a number in some form from 1 to 13. Once everything is in order, read the last letter of each title—it spells out a phrase.

Book titles shown:

- The Ten Year Dynamo
- NINE MEMBERS ONLY CLUB
- THE SEVENTH SAMURAI MONSTER
- ONE CASTLE FOREVER
- THE TWELFTH BLOCK
- A FURRY BODY AND EIGHT LEGS ASHORE
- HOW TO MAKE 6 FORTS OUT OF JELLO
- The Third rule of ABRACADABRA
- HOW TO STOP 5 POWERFUL DRAGONS WITH A CHARM
- THE MYSTERY OF THIRTEEN CURSES
- How to Make Twice the Price
- The GIANT ELEVEN FOOT POTATO
- FOUR PIRATES FOR NEVERLAND

GREAT GUTENBERG!

In the Middle Ages, most people were illiterate, but a prince would have known how to read. After the invention of the Gutenberg Press (from 1436 to 1440), regular people began to read and think for themselves without having the church or king decide what was right or wrong.

Acting the Architect

separ

rot

medit

concentr

pir

est

loc

What do you want to be when you grow up? Some people like to make buildings. To help you talk like an architect, here are some words they would use. Finish each sentence with words that end in -ate. To help you, the first part of each word is located on the roof.

HEAD CARPENTER

The word "architect" comes from the Greek for "chief builder."

We need a wall there to keep it _ _ _ _ _ _ ate

The property is a huge _ _ _ ate

With a map, it's easy to _ _ _ ate

I need to lie down and _ _ _ _ _ ate

It's a spinning door, so it needs to _ _ _ ate

When I'm drawing plans I need to _ _ _ _ _ _ _ _ ate.

He wants to live on a schooner because he's a _ _ _ ate.

Hector likes corners, so this funhouse is made up almost entirely of squares, rectangles, and triangles. Can you count how many there are?

BUILD-IT SHAPES

The most common shapes used in buildings are

triangles, rectangles, and arches,

but you can use any shape!

HERE'S A TONGUE TWISTER HECTOR LIKES TO SAY:

Hector's house has four floors four feet high.

HECTOR'S FUNHOUSE

Building Boo Boo!

Somebody has made some big mistakes constructing this building. Can you help this worker back down through the maze?

Enter

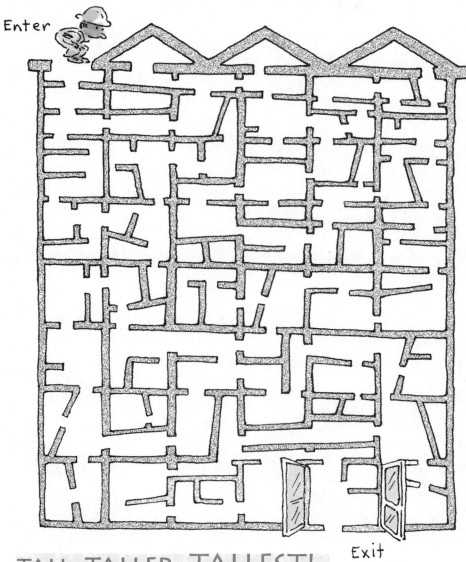

Exit

TALL, TALLER, TALLEST!

New ways of building are always being discovered, and this allows buildings to stretch ever higher. The tallest building in the world is called Burj Dubai or Dubai Tower, located in Dubai, United Arab Emirates.

People who build things use a lot of special words. Here are some words they use mixed in with other words that sound alike.* Can you match them up?

eave

leak

cellar

ceiling

stair

altar

base

pane

weight

seam

site

board

duct

road

ducked

pain

sealing

rode

leek

sight

eve

alter

stare

bored

seller

bass

seem

wait

Building Grammar

*These are homophones—words that are pronounced the same but have a different meaning or spelling.

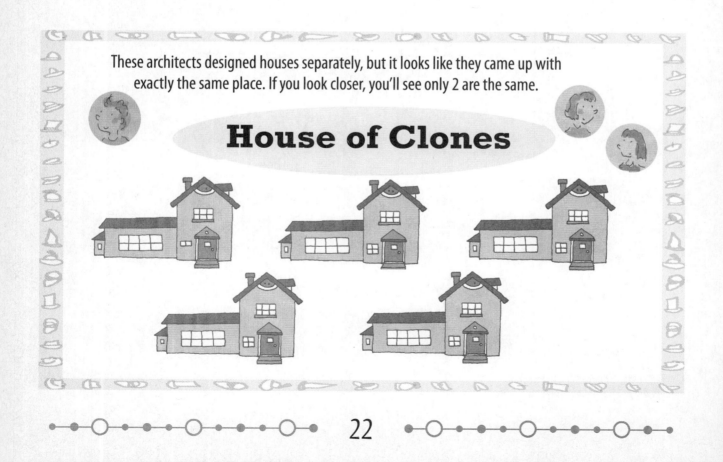

These architects designed houses separately, but it looks like they came up with exactly the same place. If you look closer, you'll see only 2 are the same.

House of Clones

WATCH YOUR STEP!

FIERY FLAMES RIDDLE

You're on a bridge in broad daylight and both directions are blocked. One way is blocked by a fire-breathing dragon. If you go the other way, there are hundreds of magnifying glasses with the sun pouring through them, and they would burn you to a crisp. How do you get off? And you can't jump, because the bridge goes over a river of fire!

When you're making a bridge, you need to know math. This engineer is trying to figure how to cross the bridge she just built, but she can only step on numbers that can be divided by 2. Can you find her route across?

YOU MADE IT!

CONFUSED COACH

These players are totally confused. The coach is showing them a new play, but he has something else on his mind. Can you see what it is?

COULD YOU COACH?

Some kids dream of growing up to play baseball, but did you ever consider being the coach? Besides being able to wear shorts and play ball all day, you could be a big influence on other kids. Sounds pretty cool!

What did the baseball glove say to the baseball?

BASEBALL HA HA!

If you were stuck in a box and only had a bat and a ball, how would you get out?

Why did the base runner pick up third and run to his house?

It's All in the Name

This baseball team has decided to call itself the Kangaroos. Sherry suggested a 9-letter name because there are 9 players on the team. Another player thought the name should also have at least 1 letter from each player's name. Can you tell who's on the team?

MICHELLE

GRAHAM

KYRA

PHIL

KANGAROOS

ALYSSA

EMMY

JORGE

DANIEL

ABDUL

JULIE

TIM

LILY

ROBERT

GLORIA

SHERRY

Baseball Biggies

Somebody has messed up these big baseball names. Can you find the correct first letter to finish their last names?

Y   C   _ANTLE   _EHRIG

P   _AYS   M   D   M

         A   _OUNG

_UTH   _USIAL   _ARON

R   _AIGE   G   M

         _IMAGGIO   _OBB

Team Twins

Like most baseball teams, the Capitals have uniforms, but only 2 are exactly the same. Can you spot them?

Regally Wrigley

Wrigley field in Chicago is one of the oldest (and most famous) baseball stadiums in the U.S. It's been home to the Chicago cubs since 1916! The stadium was built in 1914, and for 2 years housed the Federal League. Some names change and some names can be rearranged to find new names. How many words can you find in:

WRIGLEY FIELD

We found 20, but there are more!

VERY VILLE

The area surrounding the field is referred to as Wrigleyville. Ville (from the French for "town") is commonly added to many names including streets, apartments, and towns. In Finland, some boys are named Ville.

A HIVO TE LOIVO WESK OISLY THAR CHSARTMIR OVO. SUDELPH IND A ISO GEANG TI HIWIAA FES VICITAEN. ROO YEU NOXT YOIR!

Ernie Elf!

Ernie Elf

This little elf likes to play games with Santa. He's leaving a message, but it's in code. Can you figure out what he said?*

Who sings "Blue Christmas" and makes guitars?

What is the first thing elves learn in school?

How do elves greet each other?

*Exchange the letters as follows: I for A; E for O; and S for R.

A Letter to Santa

Juan has written a letter to Santa in a secret code. The only problem is he forgot to send the code breaker. Can you help Santa figure out what the letter says? Here's a hint: 4 letters are interchangeable: E for O; C for D; A for W; T for S.

DOUR TWNSW)
FER DHRITSMWT DWN
YEU BRING MO W JOS
PLUNO WND W REDKOS
THIP? I AWNS SE FLY
WREUNC SHO AERLC
WNC SHON GE SE SHO
MEEN. PLOWTO MWKO
SHOM BIG ONEUGH
FER MY FWMILY
WNC MY CEG
LELW.
SHWNK YEU
VORY MUDH,
JUWN

WHAT DID THE COW SAY ON CHRISTMAS MORNING?

Japan, a predominantly
Buddhist country, celebrates Christmas
for the same reason a lot of westerners do: they love
the gifts and colorful lights. Japanese shopping malls and
store windows are full of decorations around December 25th.

Forever Favorite Friends

Every holiday these friends get a photo taken—it's a tradition! But this year, a lot has changed. Can you spot the 12 differences?

Holiday Scramble

There are 2 things all holidays have in common. Can you unscramble the letters below to find the 2 words? Hint: both start with the letter "f."

s n r l i f e f i y a d m

HUH HOLIDAYS?

Have you heard of these wacky holidays?

August 6: Wiggle Your Toes Day

First Friday the 13th of each year: Blame Someone Else Day

August 15: Kiss and Make Up Day

February 14: Ferris Wheel Day
(Valentines Day is also celebrated)

These are other holiday words that have the letter "f" in them.

f _ _ = a great time.

_ _ f _ _ = presents.

f _ _ _ _ _ _ = another word for fun.

f _ _ _ = what you eat.

_ _ _ ff _ _ _ = what's in the turkey.

f _ _ _ _ _ _ _ = you like it the most.

FESTIVE FINANCES

MOM

Gloves $5.00

Book $5.00

Perfume $4.50

Scarf $3.00

SIS

Earrings $6.50

Socks $2.50

Hat $4.50

Game $6.00

Holidays can be expensive. Terry's Dad gave him $20 to buy gifts. He's already spent $10 and still has to get gifts for his mom and sister. What will he have to buy to use up all the money?

Bank on It!

Make a piggy bank out of a water bottle.

1. Glue paper or material around the bottle. From the material, cut ears and glue them on. To make the snout, screw on the lid.

2. Ask your mom for empty thread spools. They're perfect for legs once you paint them.

3. Get a pipe cleaner or any long material for the tail. Glue it on the back.

4. Make eyes out of paper by drawing circles with dots in them. Glue them on the face.

5. Ask a parent to cut a slot in the piggy bank's back. Remember, it has to be large enough for coins or paper money.

6. It's ready to use! All you have to do is unscrew the nose to get your money out!

Dive at Your Own Risk!

It's too late now, but this diver has just noticed he's not going to be the only one in the pool. Can you see how many fish are already swimming around here?

WET AND WILD!

Even though most cats hate water, they love fish. It is believed that the ancestors of today's house cats lived in the marshes of Egypt, where they would have hunted all kinds of water animals, including frogs and birds.

MATCH N' MIX

Everybody is coming back from swimming at once, and the wind has mixed up their caps! Can you match the hats to their owners? Careful, somehow an extra hat has blown in that doesn't belong to anyone.

SLIPPERY SAYINGS

Try saying this 5 times fast:

Six slippery snails slid slowly seaward.

MINNOW MAZE

This little minnow doesn't like being at the back of the school. Can you help him find his way to the front?

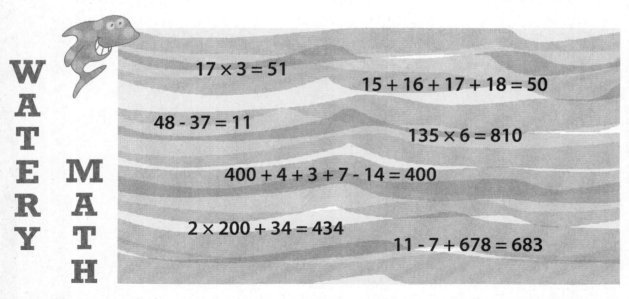

WATERY MATH

$17 \times 3 = 51$

$15 + 16 + 17 + 18 = 50$

$48 - 37 = 11$

$135 \times 6 = 810$

$400 + 4 + 3 + 7 - 14 = 400$

$2 \times 200 + 34 = 434$

$11 - 7 + 678 = 683$

Just like you, this fish is going to school. Can you help him figure out which equations don't work?

Word to the Wise

Fish swim in schools because they feel safer that way. These words are trying to find the group they belong to. Write each word in the box where it belongs.*

hockey

robot

ostrich

COUNTRY

Chile

soup

BIRD

soccer

SPORTS

owl

golf

Greece

paddle

canoe

bread

robin

baseball

balloon

phone

yacht

Australia

apple

tofu

FOOD

BOAT

ferry

tomato

Finland

steamer

sparrow

radio

football

eagle

Japan

*Careful: There are 4 words that don't belong.

Kitchen Clutter

There are 5 cooks in the kitchen. They all like to use each of the tools below, so there should be 5 of each item, but some don't show up 5 times. Can you find which ones show up 5 times?

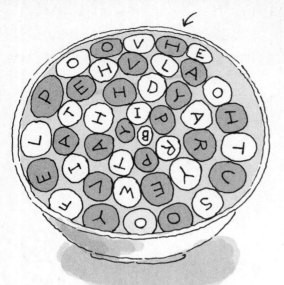

Macaroni Message

The cook has spent a lot of time arranging the letters in this pasta salad. Start on the outside with the dark-colored letters and go into the center of the bowl. When you get there, read the light-colored letters on the way out. What special message has he left?

Dragon Dessert

This dragon looks very hungry. Connect the dots to see what his favorite dessert is.

EDIBLE ILLEGIBLE

This chef is having trouble figuring out his recipe. He's looking for one name—Pasta Primavera—but only one of these has all the right letters. Can you help him find it?

AMIPRTRSVAEEPA

MIRAPTAAVPRSA

RATSRPAAMPEVA

MAIARPAPESRVAT

ARERPAASVAPMI

Everybody loves Gilles's homemade tea, but he wants to keep the ingredients a secret, so he invented a code. Can you figure out what's inside his tea?

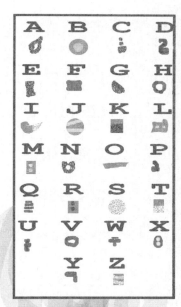

Mixin' Kitchen

This chef is confused. The foods with double letters have gotten mixed up. He needs to know their names so he can write his recipes. Can you put them back where they belong?

CALLOT

ATTLE

LEPPUCE

ZUZZHINI

DIRR PICKLE

EPPPLANT

HUSSUS

MUSHRTTM

PICCA

SPAGHEOOI

DEMMERT

BLUEBETTY

BURRER

PEGGER

CHELLY

VANIRRA

PLEASE EAT THE FLOWERS

Most salads have lettuce, but many flowers are edible. But be careful, some are poisonous!

CA _ _ OT ❖ A _ _ LE ❖ LE _ _ UCE ❖ ZU _ _ HINI ❖

DI _ _ PICKLE ❖ E _ _ PLANT ❖ HU _ _ US ❖ MUSHR _ _ M

❖ PI _ _ A ❖ SPAGHE _ _ I ❖ DE _ _ ERT ❖ BLUEBE _ _ Y ❖

BU _ _ ER ❖ PE _ _ ER ❖ CHE _ _ Y ❖ VANI _ _ A

Budget Bust-Up

Groceries can be expensive, so Jonah decided to put his family on a budget. He's put aside $100 to go shopping, but it looks like Cooper has messed things up. Can you put the pieces back together and see which 2 bag halves add up to exactly $100?

A BITE IN THE KITCHEN
What do you call a vampire that lives in the kitchen?

CHAPTER 9

DON'T I KNOW YOU?

FAMOUS FIT

These famous people have been given a pass to get into the Independent Film Awards.
One of them doesn't match the original. Can you tell who has the fake?

Lola Barns

Biff Stone

Tasha Terence

Valerie Irons

Stone Wilson

Tad Powers

FUNNY SIDE OF FAME

What do you do when there's a kidnapping?

WAKE HIM UP!

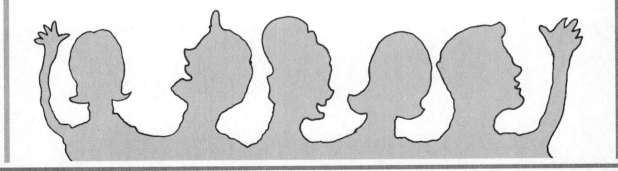

MARQUEE MIX UP

- - - - - - - - - - - -   - - - - -   - - - - - - - - -

The names of these famous people have fallen off the marquee.
Can you collect the letters and put them where they belong?

LELNEASCPELSCVTSINSAUIAIRAS

THE PRICE OF FAME

Fame may not be that desirable after all. Doctors have discovered famous
people often have more health problems due to high stress levels, anxiety, and
the pressure of the paparazzi. Maybe being a regular person isn't too bad!

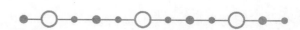

Pros and Cons

Being famous
has its pros and cons.
Which is better, fame or privacy?

All the pros are 3 or 5 words (except for one, which is 8), and
all the cons are 4 or 6 words (except for one, which is 7).

deal with large crowds of fans

have beautiful gift baskets
delivered for no reason

Get into restaurants

know famous people

make mistakes and the world knows

work far away from your family

have free clothes delivered daily

have cameras follow you
when you're jogging

receive fan mail

can't relax in public

travel world in private jets

Happy to See You!

Who has a different appearance in many countries, but wherever he goes everyone is happy to see him?

A M A S M A I P B U

K N D Y P T L Y S E

Fill in letters between the lines to form vertical 3-letter words. When you have them all, it will spell out the name of our mystery guest.

Famous Few

Not everyone is going to be famous so it is a good thing some people just want to look like their heroes. Can you tell which fan didn't get it quite right?

Bug Bug

Katie loves her messy hair. Now she's even happier—her uncle has just discovered a whole bunch of bugs have moved in! Can you count how many there are?

It has been estimated there are 10 quintillion insects alive at any one time on earth. That's **10,000, 000, 000, 000, 000, 000!**

What did the judge say when the stinkbug walked into court?

ODOR! ODOR IN THE COURT!

Insecticode

That insect looks really annoyed. Can you figure out what he's saying?

CODE

A	B	E	G	L	M	O	R	U	Y
☉	☐	◡	♡	◐	⌒	⊓	▣	⬠	⊖

I Know That Smell!

Many insects cannot see very well, so they communicate using their sense of smell. They can detect certain chemicals that tell them if other insects are male or female, or if they belong to the same species.

Fly Got Your Tongue?

Don't let these bugs bug you. Let's have some fun with some buggy tongue twisters. Can you repeat these silly sayings without losing your way?

Wild worms wiggled wildly.

Fresh French fried fly fritter.

Lucy ladybug laid low in London.

The caterpillar spilled a cart of pillows.

Fly Through Fly

This fly is small, but look at the tinier fly trying to work his way through the maze. If he doesn't make it through quietly, he could be eaten!

ENTER

END

WEB DESIGN

This spider isn't doing too well at catching his dinner, but he has caught some beautiful leaves. Can you count how many? Here's a hint: To make counting easier, color them in as you go—you'll end up with a beautiful design!

VEGGIE SPIDEE

There are about 40,000 species of spider known to man. Only 1 is a vegetarian! It is called Bagheera Kiplingi, after a character in Rudyard Kipling's The Jungle Book.

CHAPTER 11

EATING WITHOUT MEATING

FOOD FUN

P	E	A	R	R	L	R	I	C	E	O	N
T	F	A	L	O	N	A	R	G	R	L	S
O	W	S	U	B	S	S	N	H	E	S	N
N	E	F	P	E	G	A	J	M	D	A	A
U	O	K	E	A	R	W	A	P	P	L	E
T	R	U	G	O	Y	R	T	F	G	A	B
S	E	P	G	T	M	I	S	R	I	D	N
U	C	E	S	P	I	N	A	C	H	E	G
W	A	T	E	R	L	K	P	I	L	C	A
B	I	R	L	O	K	O	T	A	M	O	T

Eating healthy is a reward in itself. Can you find 16 food items that will fill you up and make you feel better? Don't be surprised if you have to turn the book around. You might find some words diagonally, backward, or even upside down!

SMART VEG

A study of thousands of women and men has shown that vegetarians have higher IQs than meat eaters (on average, 5 points higher). So, your mom was right, eat your veggies!

Eating vegetarian can be a challenge sometimes. Can you help Dean find his way through the hamburger and fast food restaurants to Vicky's Veggie Heaven?

What did the lettuce say to the celery?

Why did the tomato go out with a prune?

Why did the tomato blush?

Round Reading

Trevor likes a big juicy hamburger. He may not be too happy to see what his mom has made for dinner. Can you figure out what it is? The trick is to find where to start reading.

Hint: This will be easier to figure out if you hold it up to a mirror.

♪ Singing Supper Songs ♪

These kooky campers are singing about what they want for dinner when they get back to the cabin, but the first letters are missing. Can you fill them in and make sense of their songs?

__aked __ean __ologna __read

__old __arrot __heese __annelloni

__ried __ish __inger __ricassee

__arinated __ushy __exican __eat

__picy __almon __teak __tew

__angy __riple __oasted __ortillas

__ld __rganic __at __melet

Vicky Loves Veggies!

Vicky is going to camp and wants to make sure she has enough of her favorite foods. Can you find these in her pack? If you look closely, you'll see a surprise!*

1 watermelon · **3** pineapples · **6** carrots · **7** strawberries · **8** blueberries · **3** broccoli · **5** apples · **6** pears · **4** bananas

*For more fun, get out your crayons and color everything in.

MONDO VEGGIE

Dinosaurs were the biggest animals to roam the earth. The great majority of them were vegetarian, living off leaves and plants.

RICH AND FAMOUS

It's so old it needs to be _ _ _ lace _.

Dinner's ready, put out the _ lace _ _ _ _.

When you dress up you wear a neck _ _ _.

People love jewelry, especially necklaces. One famous necklace sold for $3.17 million! Maybe you can't afford that, but you can have fun playing with this necklace. Each word has either "neck" or "lace" in it.

He had an accident and has to wear a neck _ _ _ _ _.

Traffic is so tight there, it's a _ _ _ _ _ _ neck.

If you're the queen, you live in a _ _ lace.

I have to do some shopping at the _ _ _ _ _ _ place.

It's so nice and warm by the _ _ _ _ _ lace.

He was traveling at a _ _ _ _ _ neck speed.

It's cold outside, put on your _ _ _ _ _ _ neck sweater.

ANCIENT DRESS UP

Archaeologists have found 100,000-year-old beads worn as jewelry in North Africa. Not only were people decorating themselves, it is believed the grape-sized shells were used as symbols.

Finding Freddy

Different bodies have different markings. Sheila is looking for her crocodile Freddy. It shouldn't be too hard to find him because he has unique spots.

He must have:
* 3 bands on his tail
* a mark on his left eye only
* a dark hind foot
* a dark snout.

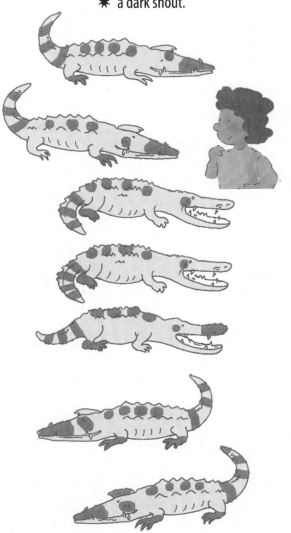

You Can Handle It!

Did you ever think of all the words that have "hand" in them? See if you can finish these sentences.

Let's go play hand_ _ _ _ after school.

This is a very hand_ _ _ _ man.

Glass needs to be hand_ _ _ carefully

If you're poor, sometimes you need a hand_ _ _.

That's one of a kind, it's hand_ _ _ _ _ _ _.

Having 4 kids is quite a hand_ _ _.

When riding your bike, always hold the hand_ _ _ _ _ _.

Look Out for That Body!

These kids love to skateboard, and they've all had a few bumps and scrapes. See if you can find the worst accident. It must have the following features:

★ It must be 2 words.

★ The second word must be 2 syllables.

★ Both words have an E.

★ Both words have a D.

BRUISED SHIN

TWISTED ANKLE

SCRAPED ELBOW

BANGED FOREHEAD

CUT FINGER

BROKEN LITTLE FINGER

A SHORT HISTORY OF SKATEBOARDING

Nobody knows who invented the first skateboard, but it is clear it started in California in the 1950s when surfers decided it would be fun to surf the roads as well as the waves!

AMAZING SENSES

Our bodies are amazing!

Think of all the things we can do.

This artist has made a list of what our senses do, but somehow they have gotten mixed up.
Can you put the number beside the correct activity?

1. SIGHT
2. SMELL
3. TASTE
4. TOUCH
5. HEARING

Turn on the radio ___

Notice something stinky ___

Pet a cat ___

Watch TV ___

Be told a secret ___

Take a photograph ___

Feel the wind ___

Inhale flowers ___

Listen to music ___

Read a book ___

Chew gum ___

Sniff old socks ___

Lick the bowl ___

Look in the mirror ___

Feel sandpaper ___

Enjoy ice cream ___

Step into a hot tub ___

Enjoy perfume ___

Put on headphones ___

Drink lemonade ___

TRIPLE TROUBLE

BETH   CAROL   KIM

"Supertwins" is a common term for triplets.

Everybody is unique, but Beth, Carol, and Kim are triplets. People often get them confused, so they try to dress differently. Study the girls for a minute, then answer the questions below to see how much you notice.

Who has a striped belt? _____ Who has longer hair? _____ Who is wearing a necklace? _____ Who isn't wearing a bracelet? _____ Who has a ring? _____ Who has horizontal dots on her bathing suit? _____ Who has a stripe on her bathing suit? _____ Who has a bandage? _____ Who has 2 buttons? _____ Who has only 1 bow on her shoe? _____ Who isn't smiling? _____

CHAPTER 13

SHADES
&
TRENCH COATS

Colorful Clues

This artist is about to give a clue to help solve which color comes next. Can you figure it out before she paints on the canvas?*

Red
Blue
Green
Yellow

Pink

Turquoise

Purple

Scarlet

*Here's a clue: It's not about the color

WHEN A SPY GOES ON VACATION, WHAT KIND OF VEHICLE DOES HE RIDE?

WALL SCRAWLS

This spy has found a cave with a message scrawled on the wall. Maybe it's a clue! Can you help her figure it out? Here's a clue: Write out the alphabet and see which letters are close to the letters in the message.

XBUDI ZPVS IFBE UIF DFJMJOH HFUT WFSZ MPX!

SAY IT WITH STONE

People have been writing on surfaces for thousands of years. Some of the earliest remaining evidence of writing is found on cave walls. It is believed cave men used sharpened stones. Symbols (of animals or planted crops) were the "language" used at this time, as there was no alphabet or letters.

Follow the Tracks

This super sleuth has made a discovery that will tie up the case. Can you follow the numbers to discover what he has found?

DID YOU KNOW?

The word "spy" comes from the French word espionage.

Eye Spy

Which pupil can always see the farthest?

Holy Hedges!

ENTER

EXIT?   EXIT?   EXIT?   EXIT?

This spy is seeing double. Can you help him find his way through the hedge maze?

A MAZE-ING HEDGES

Using hedges to make mazes dates back to Roman times. The oldest surviving hedge maze is at Hampton Court Palace in England. It was planted between 1689 and 1694.

CHAPTER 14

I LIKE ALIKE

HELPING  HEROES

These heroes have just returned from cleaning up their local beach. It looks like they found exactly the same junk, but if you look closer, it's not quite the same. There are 2 things that aren't in both bags. Can you find them?

PRECYCLING

Everyone's heard of recycling, but have you heard of precycling? It means to prevent recycling. If you use something you already have, like taking your own bag to the store, you precycle by keeping a new one from being used. If you buy cloth napkins instead of paper towels, you save the landfill. It's pretty smart! Can you think of any more?

Million Mosquito Morning

Is Ernie having a dream, or are all these mosquitoes exactly the same?

See if you can find one that is different from the others.

School Bus Scam

These kids are about to get on their school bus, but something is not quite right. Can you spot the 10 differences?

BOSTON·MA

BOSTON·

Millie and Mollie

Millie and Mollie look like identical twins...but they're not. So, it's no surprise that their toy boxes look alike but are actually full of differences. Can you spot all 10?

ANCIENT TWINS

The word "twin" comes from the ancient German word twin or twine, meaning "two together."

PICTURE PERFECT

Paul · Crystal · Pablo · Paul · Crystal · Pablo

Ellen · Suzie · Morgan · Ellen · Suzie · Morgan

Adam · Raul · Nadine · Adam · Raul · Nadine

These kids have just come back from camp, and somebody has been playing with their photos.
Can you find the changes? Now find the first letter of the 6 photos that have been altered
and rearrange them to spell out what they all have in common.

WHAT'S GREEN AND
SHORT AND GOES CAMPING?

A boy sprout!

CHAPTER 15

COLOR MIX UP

A Day at the Beach

Here's a fun project you can do on a rainy day. Imagine you're at the beach as you color in this frame and selection of things you would find at the beach. If you want, you can cut it out and make a real frame.

What do all these have in common: kite flying, bocce ball, football, volleyball, rugby, Frisbee, long jump, and foot race. They're all games you can play at the beach!

Calculate and Color

Everyone is always forgetting Anna's birthday. Can you figure out when it is from these clues?

1. The month in which she was born has 8 letters.

2. Anna was born 4 days before a big holiday.

3. The month has 31 days.

Make this birthday page more fun by coloring everything in.

What's your favorite type of birthday present?

Another birthday present!

Choosing a Color

This artist has discovered a new color, but he can't decide what to call it. The name has to have 2 Es, only 1 word with 2 syllables, 1 S, and 6 vowels.

Can you figure out which name he chose?

Sunset Serenade

Willow Mist

Powdery Park

Dusky Delight

Teatime Rose

Greenish Gold

Evening Storm

Pretty Princess

Kari is trying to figure out what her cat's favorite color is. It looks like Princess is helping. Join letter to letter and number to number to find out.

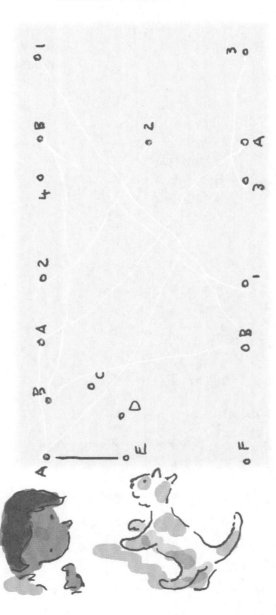

Noticing Nature

Here's a game you can play. Next time you go out to the park, see how many of these things you can see, and notice the colors! Now get coloring!

It is estimated there are 1 million insects living on every acre of land!

CHAPTER 16

FISH FRENZY

Some fish can change their markings to hide from their enemies. Imagine being able to make stripes appear on your skin!

WHALE TALE!
Why should you never trust whales with secrets?

Find-a-Fish

There are 3 types of fish that have exact twins. Can you help Kristin find them?

Seaweed Seconds

These fish have found a great seaweed field for dinner. Most have come back for seconds, thirds, and more. Can you figure out how many times each fish has eaten? Who has had the most? How many times in total have the fish eaten the seaweed?

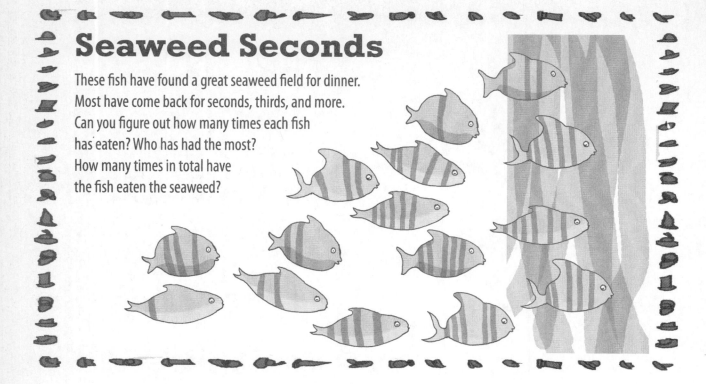

This fish has an interesting way of saying goodbye to his friends.

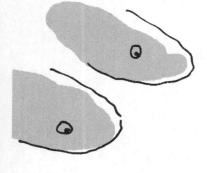

Round and Round

Can you figure out what it is? The trick is to decide where to start.

Finish a Fish

A lot of fish are disappearing from the ocean, but you can help them. Why not get some practice by bringing these ones back? Just draw the missing lines to restore them to their original form.

FISH FACT

Fish feel pain and suffer stress just like mammals and birds.

Say It Underwater!

What kind of craziness are these silly fish getting up to? Can you figure out what they're saying? All the words end with -ell or -ill.

This fish is about to have a _ _ _ ill!

Smart octopus! He makes his own ink for his _ _ ill pen.

Can you _ _ ill a drink underwater?

Loud minnow. What a big _ ell!

School has started. That's the _ ell!

Lucky eel. He just threw a penny down the _ ell.

WATERY WACKINESS!

What do you get when you cross a fish with an elephant?

What does a baby fish become after it's 3 days old?

What's the difference between a bird and a fish?

Danger in the Skies

Flying can be very dangerous, and it's not just weather that can cause trouble.

Follow the directions below and, by the process of elimination, figure out what else poses a risk in the skies.

Cross out any word that is a color, a number, rhymes with "room," has 2 Rs together, or is a sport.

TWO	DOOM	BIG	FURRY	BIRDS	ASSUME
TENNIS	NARROW	PURPLE	CAN	BORROW	TWENTY
ONE	BE	ZOOM	PARROT	JUST	YELLOW
AS	TWELVE	GREEN	GOLF	DANGEROUS	ORANGE
PRESUME	AS	BARRIER	STORMS	BROOM	SORRY
SEVEN	CARROT	WHEN	SOCCER	SEVEN	PLANES
FOOTBALL	RED	HOCKEY	ARE	BORROW	BOOM
LOOM	EIGHT	PINK	BLUE	SKIING	SKATING
FLYING	BLUE	BURROW	EIGHTEEN	GOLD	MARRY

WALK WITH CARE

According to one study, planes, trains, and automobiles are much less dangerous as ways of traveling. Guess what form of transportation is considered the most dangerous? Turn the book upside down to see.

Walking!

I Predict...

A Lot of Rain!

Mt. Waialeale in Hawaii receives 39 feet of rain per year!

1A 2B 12C 3D 4E ___

AZ BY CX DW __

BA DC FE HG JI __

MN LO KP JQ IR __

1A2 3B4 5C6 ___

We all know weather can be changeable, but some weather patterns are predictable, like the letter and number combinations above. Can you figure out what should go in the last space?

It's a Mighty Big Wave!

It appears tsunamis have been around for a long time. There are descriptions of giant waves and the sea swallowing villages in many cultures. In Australia, there is an ancient Aboriginal story of a "white wave" devastating the people. For many years, this was believed to refer to the arrival of white people, but recent evidence suggests it may refer to a tsunami.

Here are some other words with "un" in them. Can you fill in the missing letters?

When there's no clouds there's _un_ _ _ _ _ _

It's a really huge hill. _ _ un _ _ _ _

When you lift something really heavy you might make this noise. _ _ un _

It's not over, it's un _ _ _

He's married to your aunt. un _ _ _

It's where you go to have a great time. _ un _ _ _ _ _ _

It Came from Above!

Not all tsunami are caused by earthquakes. Some are caused by comets or meteorites This is called a cosmogenic tsunami.

WACKY WEATHER

This weatherman made a big mistake in his forecast. Now he has to get out of here! Can you help him get back to the news station while avoiding the tornadoes and snowstorms?

COMICAL CLIMATE

Why do you have to be careful when it rains cats and dogs?

Why did the lady go outside with her purse wide open?

UNDERWATER WEATHER

There's weather underwater, too! Scientists have discovered there are waves and currents that sweep across the sea very much like wind and storms move through the air.

Weather Permitting

This pilot looks like he's in for some bumpy weather, but if he's careful he can make it through to the airport. You can help him, but you have to know the clues. You can go anywhere there is a sun. If there is no sun, you have to turn back! No traveling diagonally, but you can go up, down, or side to side. Hold on!

start

finish

Weathery Words

Can you match the weather term with the meaning?

BLUSTERY
PRECIPITATION   tropical cyclone
SLEET
STRATUS   rain   ice pellets
HURRICANE   hot summer weather
DOG DAYS   windy   a type of cloud

Musical Mayhem

Fluffy loves good music, but what do you do when your owner is still learning? Join the dots and see what Fluffy has to listen to.

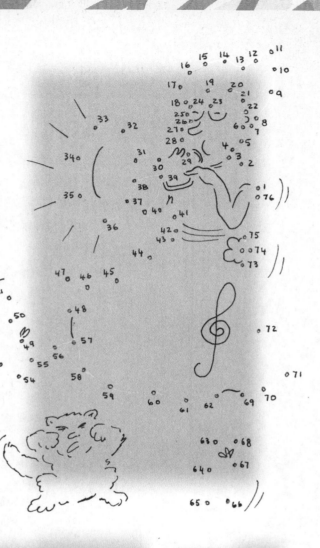

Make Your Own Kind of Music

Here's an instrument you can make at home. You'll need:

* pen
* rubber band
* wax paper
* paper towel roll

With the pen, punch a series of holes along the side of the roll. Secure the wax paper over one end of the paper towel roll with the rubber band. To play, sing a tune into the open end of your new horn!

Hide n' Seek Songs

Brendan has 2 hobbies. One is writing music, and the other is learning about animals. He's decided to combine the two by writing fun sayings with animals hidden in them. How many can you spot?

Thor sent a thunderbolt through the sky.

There's an energetic owl on the loose.

The cups were lined up in a plastic row.

I hit my thumb early in the morning.

Tony could be a very convincing actor.

We've all made errors now and then, dear.

The criminal was a deaf rogue on the run.

Pull a match out of your sleeve.

The bull ambled to the garden gate.

Mummy Music
What kind of music do mummies like?

No I Don't Want You Without Me!

There's a new musical in town called "Land of Opposites." Everyone means the opposite of what they say.
See if you can figure out this kooky song! Write the opposite of the underlined words.

We must <u>walk</u> <u>towards</u> to
<u>end</u> an <u>old</u> life in our <u>ugly</u> <u>old</u>
home. I <u>won't</u> keep you <u>cold</u> and
<u>wet</u> from <u>night</u> til <u>morning</u>!

<u>No</u> I <u>don't</u> want you <u>without</u> me!
We belong <u>apart</u> <u>over</u> the <u>sun</u>. <u>My</u>
eyes are so <u>tiny</u> and <u>dark</u> I <u>couldn't</u>
look at <u>me</u> the rest of <u>your</u> life!

I'M A WRITER!

Write your own song.
It can be about anything!
Here are a few ideas to
get you started.

Your best friend
Your nose
School
Sports
Your pet

WHAT KIND OF MUSIC DID
THE PILGRIMS LISTEN TO?
Plymouth Rock!

Secret Song

Everyone has a favorite musical instrument. Elise likes to tell us in code what hers is. Take the first letter of each line and rearrange the letters to find out what she likes to play.

Once a week
I go to school to
Practice music
And sing some
New songs.

Special Stage

This singer needs a special location to sing her songs. Can you connect the dots to see her favorite place to sing?

Sing Song Spy

This songwriter wants to make sure nobody copies her material until she hits the stage. Can you see what she's writing about?*

for the masquerade ball.
to Carnegie Hall
I can fly out east
When my song's released
with my great new sound.
I'm undercover
So you must know why
I'm a singing spy

*Here's a hint: Turn the book upside down and look in a mirror.

HOW TO WRITE A SONG

1. Think of a subject you know about
2. Imagine talking to your best friend
3. Do an online search for rhyming words
4. Tell your story
5. Have fun!

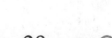

Polar Predicament

The ice is melting so fast this polar bear might not make it back to shore.
Can you help her through the maze and back to safety?

In the wild, polar bears can live up to 25 years.

Human beings are the polar bears' only predator.

Polar bears have been known to swim 100 miles.

The polar bear is the world's largest predator.

Adult males can measure up to 10 feet.

It is believed there are between 20,000 and 25,000 polar bears.

Sleepy Surprise

This little bear is enjoying his winter hibernation, but it looks like somebody else snuck in while he was asleep. Connect the dots to see who it is.

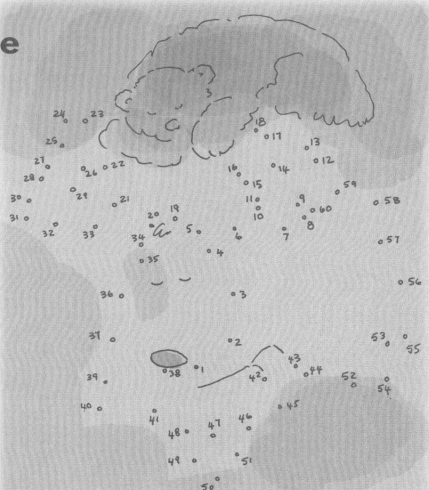

Spring Full of Surprises

Something else is hiding here. Can you see what this bear will be when he wakes up? Cross out every letter that is not E, P, U, I, R, D, S to see what the bear's reaction will be.

S G W O O K L U T O R A P
Y O R J I M N K O A W L L
B S Q N L E X L W B D O X

Spot the Spots

No two giraffes have the same spot pattern, but it looks like somebody was cloned here. Can you find the giraffe that shows up twice?

Wildly Tame

Mammals are everywhere on earth and they come in all shapes and sizes. Can you match the following words with their opposites?

humble	cute
ferocious	tall
energized	bald
short	quiet
loud	cuddly
ugly	tame
furry	lazy
prickly	fierce
friendly	majestic

The Fox and the Farmer

It looks like trouble in the valley. This farmer has to get his flock back home, but first he needs to scare the fox away. How will he get through the herd of sheep?

enter

exit

How do sheep keep warm in the winter?

FARM FUNNIES

Which dance will a sheep not do?

How do chickens dance?

What do you give a sick pig?

Where do milkshakes come from?

CROSSWORDINOSAUR

The big dinosaurs would never have been able to hide in the bushes, but some dinosaurs were so tiny they would have made a chicken look big.

```
D I N D I N O S D R
R O R U A S O N I D
I D U O S U A N N D
R S A U D O S I O N
S A S S O N S A S O
D I O D I N O S A S
D I N O S A U R U U
S D I N O S A U R A
D I D N O S A U R R
```

Can you find the 5 times "dinosaurs" appears here?

NEMICOLOPTERUS

This is a big name for one of the smallest dinosaurs ever discovered. Similar in size to a sparrow, it was a gliding dinosaur with a wingspan of about 10 inches. It is believed this tiny Pterodactyl lived on insects.

Different Dinosaurs

A lot has changed since dinosaurs roamed the earth, and a lot has changed in these 2 pictures. Can you spot the 12 differences?

Dino Quiz

Are the following statements true or false?

___ There were some flying dinosaurs.

___ Dinosaurs could not swim.

___ The oldest dinosaur remains are 100 million years old.

___ We do not know what color dinosaurs were.

___ Dinosaurs were mostly meat eaters.

Dino Gathering

These dinosaurs are coming to a party, but somebody has to keep count. Can you figure out the following?

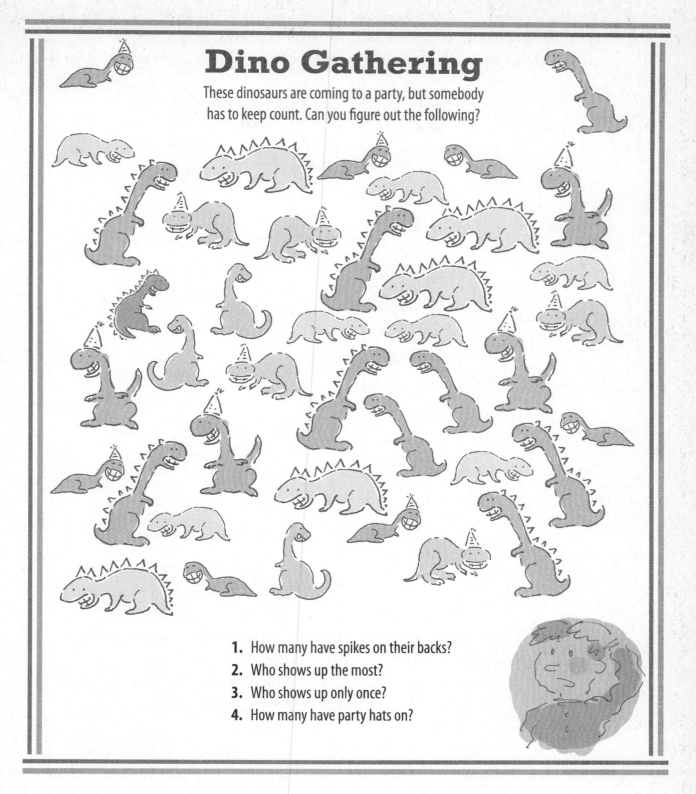

1. How many have spikes on their backs?
2. Who shows up the most?
3. Who shows up only once?
4. How many have party hats on?

Dinosaurs weren't known for being the smartest reptiles that ever lived, so this big guy has his work cut out for him. Can you help him find his way back to the swamp he calls home?

HOME SWEET HOMEASAUR

SMARTER THAN YOUR AVERAGE WALNUT

There is no exact way to measure dinosaurs' intelligence, but scientists have a theory that measures the brain as compared with body size. Humans are at the top of the pile and dinosaurs are in the lowest levels. One of the first dinosaurs to be unearthed (a stegosaurus) had a brain about the size of a walnut.

Alien Audio

What if aliens landed on Earth and they were friendly? Matt's making friends with Zork, but they're having trouble communicating. Zork's transponder is mixing up the letters in each word. Can you put them back in order and see what he's saying?

> *I nac mupj tiffy efet ghih! No ym telpan, I dulco mupj revo royu shoeu. Ecom iistv em, ew veah on vatiygr reeth.*

MORE STARS IN THE UNIVERSE

Scientists have determined there are more stars in the universe than there are grains of sand on earth. Ten times as many, in fact, and that only includes the part of the universe visible to us. The number given is 70 sextillion—that's a 7 followed by 22 zeros. That's astronomical!

Astro Knowledge

This astronaut is reading a letter sent from NASA, but it's also a code for things he'll need to bring. He's going on a long mission, so he'll need something to keep him busy. Write down the capital letters in order. The tricky part is knowing where to put the spaces.

NASA

i hope you enjoy your spACe
jouRney Over ruSSia and the
Western wORlD. Please tell
Us if you feel diZZy at all.
wE plAN To have you home
wIthin eiGht days. yOuR
fAmily sends their loVe and
kIsses.   Thank You and
PlEase write sooN.

HOUSTON WE HAVE SNACKTIME!

What are the top 5 foods astronauts enjoy in space?
**potato chips ★ soft drinks ★ pizza ★ ice cream ★
shrimp cocktail ★ M+Ms ★ lemonade ★ steak
★ fish ★ pudding ★ tortillas ★ brownies**

We know so little about space. Just imagine what some other life forms could look like. There could even be something out there that looks like this!

Too Scary to Be True!

Found in Space

Can you imagine floating in space, trying to find the earth? Here's a much easier task: Find all 8 planets in this letter puzzle.

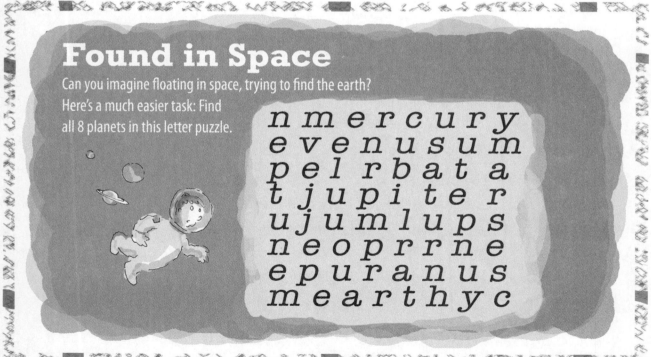

```
n m e r c u r y
e v e n u s u m
p e l r b a t a
t j u p i t e r
u j u m l u p s
n e o p r r n e
e p u r a n u s
m e a r t h y c
```

Space for Two

These astronauts all want to go to space, but there is only room for 2. Can you see who will go based on these requirements?

Each astronaut must:

1. Be wearing a pack
2. Not wear glasses
3. Be wearing boots
4. Have no belt on
5. Have a flag on their shoulder
6. Have only 2 hearts on them.

SPACE STUFF

✦ Out of 195 astronauts, 123 were scouts when they were younger. It's not a guarantee you'll get in, but it sure could help.

✦ Keep eating your veggies, because you have to be between 58.5 and 76 inches in height to be an astronaut.

✦ On average, NASA receives about 4,000 applications every 2 years to fill 20 positions.

FUN FUR

Charlie has been outside playing all day, and it looks like he's brought a few things home. Can you see what's hiding in his fur?

CHECK IT OUT!

Taking your pets to the vet for regular checkups is a good idea. Remember, they can't tell you if anything is bothering them!

Let's Look at Luck

People have had cats as pets for thousands of years, but some people believe black cats are unlucky. Can you see 5 other things that are considered unlucky? To make sure our luck is balanced, find the 5 lucky things in the scene, too.

LUCKY OR UNLUCKY?

Different cultures consider different animals lucky or unlucky. For many Native Americans, the bear is believed to bring good fortune. Japanese consider the Maneki Neko or Beckoning Cat to be a good omen. Poor crows and ravens have been considered unlucky for centuries.

Lookalike Litter

This litter has gotten out of hand. Of the 16 puppies shown, can you find 2 that are not alike?

MILL MONEY

You might have heard of puppy mills—places that churn out puppies for money. There are also small animal mills that breed animals like rabbits, guinea pigs, and mice. Go to the ASPCA to adopt a pet if you want to be sure you're not supporting a small animal mill.

Ollie's Gone!

Where is Ollie going? It looks like he has left a special message. Cross out every letter that is not C, E, G, H, I, J, N, O, R, S, T, U to see what he has to say.

B A P G Y W K F A B O M M P Y M Q
N L F E P A B T L V W O W J D A A L
O P W I Z F N A P W X T A B H M M
Y Z E L C P M A A I X W D A R B D C
L L U F F Y D B A A V Q S Y Z A L M

Planning Ahead

It looks like Ollie was thinking ahead. Can you see what his request is? Rearrange these letters to form 2 words.

Dirty Captain Pugwash

Dirty Captain Pugwash is leaving a message for his wife, but it looks like he's getting his letters mixed up. Can you figure out what it says? Here's a hint: He's switching (both ways) I for O; N for P; and D for S.

FLYING FUNNY

Why do seagulls fly over the sea?

Because if they flew over the bay they'd be bagels!

WOLL NOCK UN BREAS APS MOLK, BUT O MOGHT VODOT OPSOA & CHOPA, TII. SIP'T WAOT UN!

NUGDY

SEA SMARTS

Pirates weren't known to be the smartest sailors at sea. But one pirate by the name of Blackbeard was known to have great intelligence along with his ability to read and write. Although he wasn't the most fearsome, he became the most famous, having many books written and movies made about him since he died in 1718.

Although pirates didn't have to rely on spelling too much, they liked to know the basics. Since they're caught in the doldrums, they might as well have a spelling test.

All the words are missing a letter or letters, but the letters missing are silent ones. Can you figure out where they go?

nife neumonia **dout**
k p b b

num **clim** casle **nee** yat
b t k ch m

autun Lincon **woud** asma
l l th w

anser sord **sofen** hansome
w t d

This evil pirate has stationed himself at the mouth of the bay to control who comes and goes. If travelers can't figure out the clues, they might pay with their lives! Can you see where the real bomb lies?

Pass Ye Who Dare!

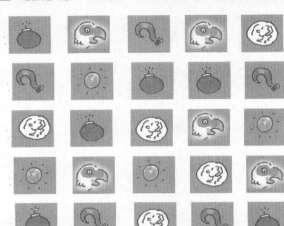

1. The real bomb is in the column with a hook in it.
2. The real bomb has a coin diagonal to it.
3. The real bomb has a parrot above and below it.

Don't forget, mateys— September 19 is Talk Like a Pirate Day!

Learning the Lingo

In case you run into a pirate, you might want to learn some of the lingo. Can you match the word with its proper meaning?

a mop

Swab

hello

Doubloon

a raised deck at the stern of a ship

Poop Deck

Hornswoggle

a gold coin   Ahoy   *to hoax or trick*

someone who does not go to sea

Landlubber

Patricia Loves Pirates

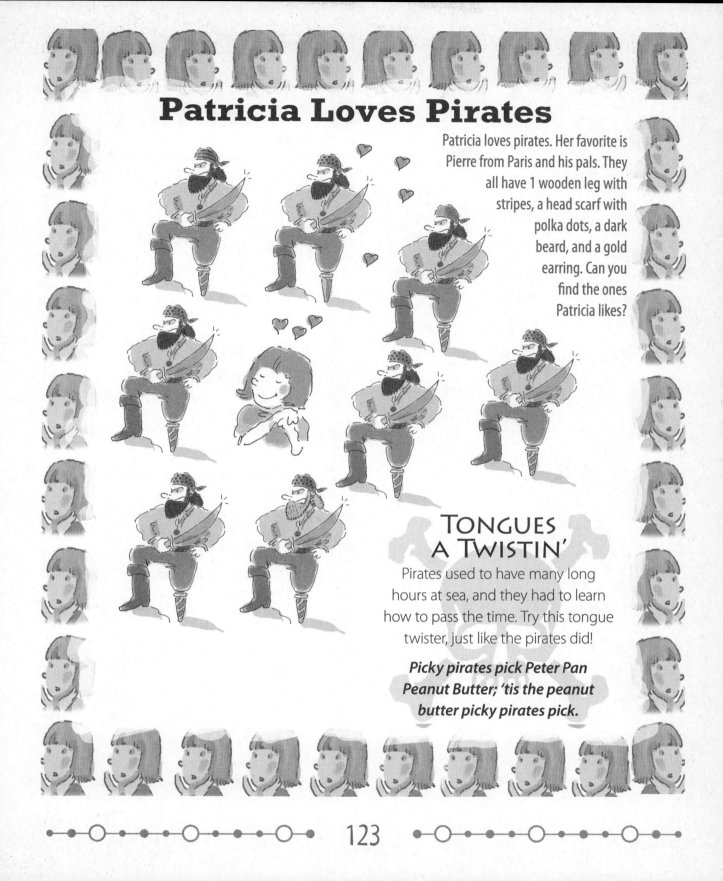

Patricia loves pirates. Her favorite is Pierre from Paris and his pals. They all have 1 wooden leg with stripes, a head scarf with polka dots, a dark beard, and a gold earring. Can you find the ones Patricia likes?

TONGUES A TWISTIN'

Pirates used to have many long hours at sea, and they had to learn how to pass the time. Try this tongue twister, just like the pirates did!

Picky pirates pick Peter Pan Peanut Butter; 'tis the peanut butter picky pirates pick.

These pirates look alike, but they're not.
Can you find the 10 differences?

PIRATE

ALIKE

Where's the Arrr?

You know these are pirates talking because all the words have "ar" in them. In fact, 1 word even has 2 "ar"s!

1. When you get a good deal, it's a _ ar _ _ _ _.

2. At night, the horses are kept in the _ ar _.

3. That's not small, it's _ ar _ _.

4. Rabbits like to munch on _ ar _ _ _ _.

5. We grow vegetables in our _ ar _ _ _.

6. Another name for a rabbit is a _ ar _.

7. It's not butter, it's _ ar _ ar _ _ _.

8. The bird on a pirate's shoulder is a _ ar _ _ _.

PUZZLE ANSWERS

Introduction

Did you find all the puzzles Max was hiding in? Max appears in:

Chapter 1: Eeeky Creepy!

Threeosaurus Hideaway • page 2

Forgetful Dr. Frankenstein • page 3

Gertrude's Game • page 4

GRUESOME: see, seem, rose, sore, gore, rug, merge, ruse, some, gem, more, morgue

VAMPIRE: mire, reap, ape, pear, mare, pare, map, pair

GRAVEYARD: year, dear, rear, grade, yard, ray, rare, gear, very, vary, grey

Joke answer: Lazybones

Spooky Spider • page 5

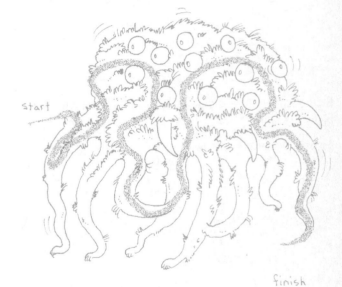

Riddle answer: Most spiders have fangs

Stinky Stuff • page 5

Old Socks, Milk, Dirty Feet, Armpits, Fish

Critter Chaos • page 6

Grape Flea Beetle, Greenstriped Mapleworm, Mimosa Webworm, Pea Weevil

So Silly • page 6

Purple parrots play proudly
Slow snakes slide south
My mother mixes monkey music
Children carefully choose cheese
Bossy bugs build barricades

PUZZLE ANSWERS

Chapter 2: Hey, What's Wrong?
Funny Flags • page 8

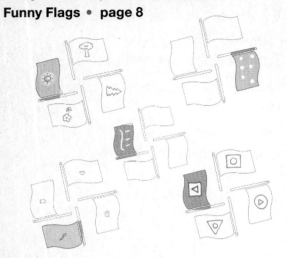

Riddle answer: A vexillologist is a person who studies the history of flags.

Hurry Harbor • page 9

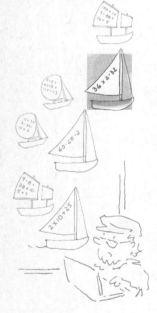

$36 \times 2 - 32 = 40$

Mussel Mix Up • page 9

Medieval Mix Up • page 10

Surreal Sights • page 11

PUZZLE ANSWERS

Chapter 3: PDU (Princess Dragon Unicorn)
Happy Princess • page 13

1. There are 3 crowns
2. There are 2 shoes on the floor
3. "How to be a Princess"
4. Stripes
5. Cat
6. An umbrella
7. A teapot
8. A balloon

Lucky 7 • page 14

Lonely Dragon • page 15

Riddle answer: To get to the other slide!

Mythical Mystery • page 16

Hello! I am a unicorn!

Smart as a Prince • page 17

One Castle Forever

How to Make Twice the Price!

The Third Rule of Abracadabra

Four Pirates in Neverland

How to Stop 5 Powerful Dragons with a Charm

How to Make 6 Forts Out of Jello

The Seventh Samurai Monster

A Furry Body and Eight Legs Ashore

Nine Members Only Club

The Ten-Year Dynamo

The Giant Eleven-Foot Potato

The Twelfth Block

The Mystery of Thirteen Curses

Phrase: READ MORE BOOKS

Chapter 4: Ladders and Stairs:
Acting the Architect • page 19

We need a wall to keep it separate.

The property is a huge estate.

With a map, it's easy to locate.

I need to lie down and meditate.

It's a spinning door, it needs to rotate.

When I'm drawing plans I need to concentrate.

He wants to live on a schooner because he's a pirate.

Hector's Funhouse • page 20

There are 7 triangles, 11 squares, and 6 rectangles.

PUZZLE ANSWERS

Building Boo Boo! • page 21

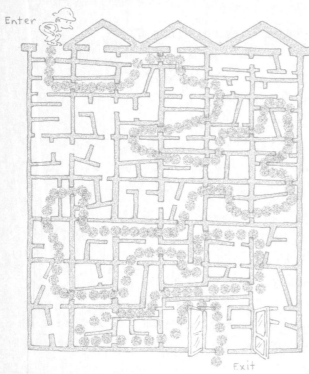

Building Grammar • page 22

eave—eve
leak—leek
cellar—seller
stair—stare
ceiling—sealing
altar—alter
base—bass
pane—pain

seam—seem
road—rode
board—bored
ceiling—sealing
site—sight
duct—ducked
weight—wait

House of Clones • page 22

Watch Your Step! • page 23

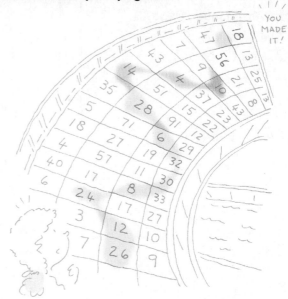

Riddle answer: You wait for the sun to go down then head toward the magnifying glasses.

Chapter 5: Batter Up!
Confused Coach • page 25

Riddle answers:

Catch you later.

Take 3 swings: 1 strike, 2 strikes, 3 strikes you're out!

The coach told him to steal third and go home.

PUZZLE ANSWERS

It's All in the Name • page 26

Kyra, Alyssa, Daniel, Jorge, Abdul, Graham, Robert, Gloria, and Sherry are all on the team.

Baseball Biggies • page 27

Ruth, Mays, Paige, Cobb, Young, Mantle, Aaron, Gehrig, Dimaggio, Musial

Team Twins • page XX

Regally Wrigley • page 28

Glee, fed, ride, glide, fled, flee, wide, wife, lied, weed, reed, yell, dig, wig, fig, feed, file, filed, defile, fried

Chapter 6: Hooray Holiday Everyday!

Ernie Elf • page 30

I have to leave work early this Christmas Eve. Rudolph and I are going to Hawaii for vacation. See you next year! Ernie Elf

Joke answers:
The elf-abet
Elfis
Small world, isn't it!

A Letter to Santa • page 31

Dear Santa,

For Christmas can you bring me a jet plane and a rocket ship? I want to fly around the world and then go to the moon. Please make them big enough for my family and my dog Lola.

Thank you very much,
Juan

Joke answer: Mooey Christmas!

Forever Favorite Friends • page 32

Huh Holidays • page 33

These are other holiday words that have the letter 'f' in them
F **un** = a great time. F **ood** = what you eat.
 gifts = present. **stu**F F**ing** = what's in the turkey.
F**estive** = another word for fun. F **avorite** = you like it the most

Holiday Scramble Answer: FAMILY FRIENDS • **page 32**

Festive Finances • page 34

If Terry buys his mom the $3.00 scarf and his sister the $2.50 socks and $4.50 hat, he will use up all $10.

Chapter 7: In the Swim

Dive at Your Own Risk • page 36

There are 12 fish

PUZZLE ANSWERS

Match n' Mix • page 37

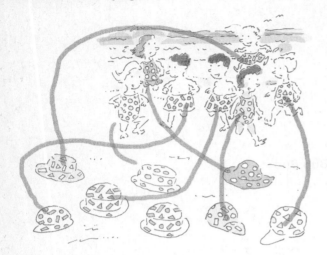

Minnow Maze • page 38

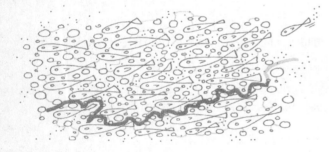

Watery Math • page 38

$15 + 16 + 17 + 18 = 49$

$11 - 7 + 678 = 682$

Word to the Wise • page 39

SPORTS: hockey, golf, baseball, soccer, football
BIRD: ostrich, owl, robin, sparrow, eagle
COUNTRY: Chile, Greece, Japan, Australia, Finland
BOAT: canoe, yacht, paddle, steamer, ferry
FOOD: tofu, apple, soup, bread, tomato

Chapter 8: Cook n' Stew
Kitchen Clutter • page 41

Macaroni Message • page 42

Hope you have a very happy birthday with lots of love

Dragon Dessert • page 42

Edible Illegible • page 43

MAIARPAPESRVAT

Top Tea Secret • page 43

Honey, mint, and coconut

PUZZLE ANSWERS

Mixin' Kitchen • page 44

CARROT, APPLE, LETTUCE, ZUCCHINI, DILL PICKLE,
EGGPLANT, HUMMUS, MUSHROOM, PIZZA, SPAGHETTI,
DESSERT, BLUEBERRY, BUTTER, PEPPER, CHERRY, VANILLA

Budget Bust Up • page 45

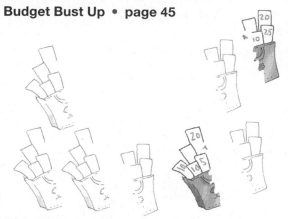

Joke answer: Spatula

Chapter 9: Don't I Know You?

Famous Fit •
page 47

Lola Barns   Biff Stone   Tasha Terence

Valerie Irons   Stone Wilson   Tad Powers

Marquee Mix Up • page 48

Princess Leia
Elvis
Santa Claus

Pros and Cons • page 49

PROS: get into restaurants, receive fan mail, have free clothes delivered daily,
travel world in private jets, know famous people, have beautiful gift baskets
delivered for no reason CONS: Can't relax in public, work far away from your
family, deal with large crowds of fans, make mistakes and the world knows,
have cameras follow you when you're jogging

Happy to See You! • page 50

AMASMAIPBU
SANTACLAUS
KNDYP TLYSE

Famous Few • page 50

**Chapter 10: I Love It
When You Bug Me!**
Bug Bug •
page 52

There are 13 bugs in Katie's hair

Insecticode • page 53

You really bug me!!

Fly Through Fly • page 54

PUZZLE ANSWERS

Web Design • page 55

There are 26 leaves.

Chapter 11: Eating Without Meating

Food Fun • page 57

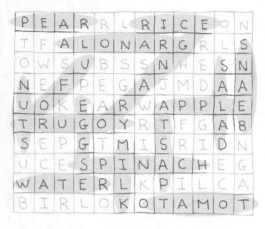

Pear, rice, granola, orange, beans, salad, nuts, tofu, yogurt, apple, salad, spinach, milk, water, pasta, tomato

Veggie Adventures • page 58

Joke answers: Are you stalking me?
Because he couldn't find a date!
Because he saw the salad dressing.

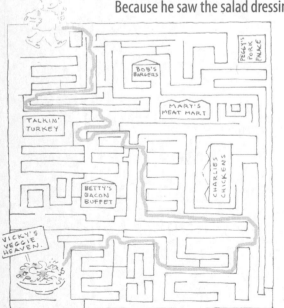

Round Reading • page 59

Soybean Surprise

Singing Supper Songs • page XX

Baked Bean Bologna Bread
Cold Carrot Cheese Cannelloni
Fried Fish Finger Fricassee
Marinated Mushy Mexican Meat
Spicy Salmon Steak Stew
Tangy Triple Toasted Tortillas
Old Organic Oat Omelet

Vicky Loves Veggies!
• page XX

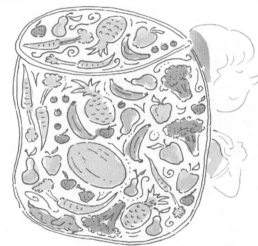

Chapter 12: Inside Outside

Rich and Famous • page 62

It's so old it needs to be replaced.
Dinner's ready, put out the placemats.
When you dress up you put on a necktie.
Traffic is so tight there is a bottleneck.
He had an accident and has to wear a neck brace.
If you're the queen you live in a palace.
I have to do some shopping at the marketplace.
It's so nice and warm by the fireplace.
He was traveling at breakneck speed.
It's cold outside, put on your turtleneck.

PUZZLE ANSWERS

Finding Freddy •
page 63

You Can Handle It! • **page 63**

Let's go play handball after school.
This is a very handsome man.
Glass needs to be handled carefully.
If you're poor, sometimes you need a handout.
That's one of a kind, it's handcrafted.
Having four kids is quite a handful.
When riding your bike, always hold the handlebars.

Look Out for That Body! • **page 64**

BANGED FOREHEAD

Amazing Senses! • **page 65**

Turn on the radio: 5	Chew gum: 3
Notice something stinky: 2	Sniff old socks: 2
Pet a cat: 4	Lick the bowl: 3
Watch TV: 1	Look in the mirror: 1
Be told a secret: 5	Feel sandpaper: 4
Take a photograph: 1	Enjoy ice cream: 3
Feel the wind: 4	Step into a hot tub: 4
Inhale flowers: 2	Enjoy perfume: 2
Listen to music: 5	Put on headphones: 5
Read a book: 1	Drink lemonade: 3

Triple Trouble • **page 66**

BETH: wears a necklace, has a stripe on her bathing suit, has only 2 buttons, has only 1 bow on her shoe

CAROL: has longer hair, isn't wearing a bracelet, has horizontal dots on her bathing suit, has a bandage

KIM: has a striped belt, has a ring, isn't smiling

Chapter 13: Shades and Trench Coats

Colorful Clues • **page 68**

Scarlet (Scarlet is 7 letters, so it comes after the 6-letter word "yellow")

Riddle answer: A spycycle!

Wall Scrawls • **page 69**

Watch your head the ceiling gets very low!

Follow the Tracks • **page 70**

Joke answer:
The one in your eye.

Holy Hedges •
page 71

PUZZLE ANSWERS

Chapter 14: I Like Alike
Helping Heroes • page 73

Million Mosquito Morning • page 74

School Bus Scam • page 74

Millie and Mollie • page 75

Picture Perfect • page 76

Crystal, Adam, Morgan, Pablo, Ellen, Raul—CAMPER

Chapter 15: Color Mix Up
Calculate and Color • page 79

Anna was born on December 21.

Choosing a Color • page 80

Teatime Rose

Pretty Princess • page 80

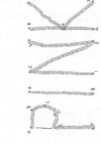

Chapter 16: Fish Frenzy
Find-a-Fish • page 83

Because they're all blubber mouths!

PUZZLE ANSWERS

Seaweed Seconds • page 84

55 times in total

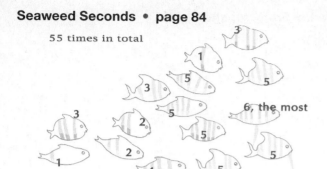

6, the most

Round and Round • page 84

SEA YOU AROUND

Say it Underwater! • page 86

This fish is about to have a thrill!
Smart octopus! He makes his own ink for his quill pen.
Can you spill a drink underwater?
Loud minnow. What a big yell!
School has started. That's the bell!
Lucky eel. He just threw a penny down the well.

Watery Wackiness • page 86

Swimming trunks
4 days old
A bird can fish but a fish can't bird!

Chapter 17: How's the Weather Up There?

Danger in the Skies • page 88

TWO	DOOM	BIG	FURRY	BIRDS	ASSUME
TENNIS	NARROW	PURPLE	CAN	BORROW	TWENTY
ONE	BE	ZOOM	PARROT	JUST	YELLOW
AS	TWELVE	GREEN	GOLF	DANGEROUS	ORANGE
PRESUME	AS	BARRIER	STORMS	BROOM	SORRY
SEVEN	CARROT	WHEN	SOCCER	SEVEN	PLANES
FOOTBALL	RED	HOCKEY	ARE	BORROW	BOOM
LOOM	EIGHT	PINK	BLUE	SKIING	SKATING
FLYING	BLUE	BURROW	EIGHTEEN	GOLD	MARRY

Big birds can be just as dangerous as storms when planes are flying.

I Predict... • page 89

1A 2B 12C 3D 4E **34F**

AZ BY CX DW **EV**

BA DC FE HG JI **LK**

MN LO KP JQ IR **HS**

1A2 3B4 5C6 **7D8**

It's a Mighty Big Wave • page 90

Sunshine, Mountain, Grunt, Under, Uncle, Funhouse

Wacky Weather • page 91

Joke answers: Because you might step in a poodle.
She expected some change in the weather.

Weather Permitting • page 92

PUZZLE ANSWERS

Weathery Words • page 92

Blustery—windy
Precipitation—rain
Sleet—ice pellets
Stratus—a type of cloud
Hurricane—tropical cyclone
Dog Days—hot summer weather

Chapter 18: Hummin' Hoedown!
Musical Mayhem •
page 94

Hide n' Seek Songs • page 95

T**hor se**nt a thunderbolt through the sky. **horse**
I hit my thum**b ear**ly in the morning. **bear**
There's an energeti**c ow**l on the loose. **cow**
The cups were lined up in a plasti**c row**. **crow**
Tony could **be a ver**y convincing actor. **beaver**
We've all ma**de er**rors now and then dear. **deer**
The criminal was a dea**f rog**ue on the run. **frog**
Pu**ll a ma**tch out of your sleeve. **llama**
The bu**ll amb**led to the garden gate. **lamb**

Joke answer: Wrap!

No I Don't Want You Without Me! • page 96

We must run away to start a new life in our beautiful new home. I will keep you warm and dry from morning til night!

Yes I do want you with me! We belong together under the moon. Your eyes are so big and bright I could look at you the rest of my life!

Secret Song • page 97
PIANO

Special Stage • page 97

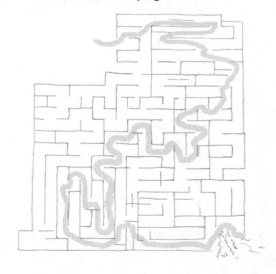

Sing Song Spy • page 98

I'm a singing spy
So you must know why
I'm underground
with my great new sound.
When my song's released
I can fly out east
to Carnegie Hall
for the masquerade ball!

Chapter 19: Flying Fur
Polar Predicament • page 100

PUZZLE ANSWERS

Sleepy Surprise •
page 101

Surprised

Spot the Spots •
page 102

Wildly Tame • **page 102**

ferocious—tame
loud—quiet
friendly—fierce
cuddly—prickly
cute—ugly
furry—bald
tall—short
lazy—energized
majestic—humble

The Fox and the Farmer •
page 103

Joke answers: How do sheep keep warm in the winter? Central bleating!

What dance will a sheep not do? The foxtrot.

How do chickens dance? Chick to chick.

What do you give a sick pig? Oinkment.

Where do milkshakes come from? Excited cows.

Chapter 20:
Dino-Might!
Crosswordinosaur •
page 105

Different Dinosaurs • **page 106**

DINO QUIZ:

False. No dinosaurs could fly.

True. Dinosaurs could not swim, but some hunted in the water.

False. The oldest dinosaur remains are 230 millions old.

True. No evidence of skin color remains.

False. Most dinosaurs were vegetarians.

PUZZLE ANSWERS

Dino Gathering • page 107

This dinosaur shows up only once.

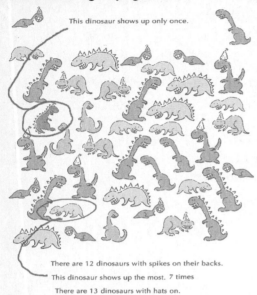

There are 12 dinosaurs with spikes on their backs.
This dinosaur shows up the most. 7 times
There are 13 dinosaurs with hats on.

Home Sweet Homeasaur • page 108

Chapter 21: Big BIG Space
Alien Audio • page 110

I can jump fifty feet high! On my planet, I could jump over your house. Come visit me, we have no gravity there.

Astro Knowledge • page 111

A CROSSWORD PUZZLE ANTIGRAVITY PEN

Top 5 foods astronauts request are: shrimp cocktail, lemonade, steak, M+Ms, and brownies.

Too Scary to Be True! • page 112

Found in Space! • page 112

Space for Two • page 113

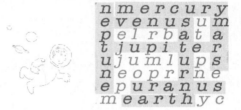

Chapter 22: PETerrific!
Fun Fur • page 115

PUZZLE ANSWERS

Let's Look at Luck • page 116

 Unlucky Lucky

Lookalike Litter • page 117

Ollie's Gone! • page 118

GONE TO JOIN THE CIRCUS

```
B A P G Y W K F A B O M M P Y M Q
N L F E P A B T L V W O W J D A A L
O P W I Z F N A P W X T A B H M M
Y Z E L C P M A A I X W D A R B D C
L L U F F Y D B A A V Q S Y Z A L M
```

SEND FOOD

Chapter 23: Pirate Powrrr!

Dirty Captain Pugwash • page 120

Will pick up bread and milk, but I might visit India & China, too. Don't wait up! Pugsy

Spell P-I-R-A-T-E • page 121

knife, pneumonia, doubt, numb, climb, castle, knee, yacht, autumn, Lincoln, would, asthma, answer, sword, soften, handsome

Pass Ye Who Dare! • page 122

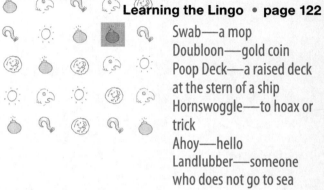

Learning the Lingo • page 122

Swab—a mop
Doubloon—gold coin
Poop Deck—a raised deck at the stern of a ship
Hornswoggle—to hoax or trick
Ahoy—hello
Landlubber—someone who does not go to sea

Patricia Loves Pirates • page XX

Pirate Alike • page 124

Where's the Arrr? • page 124

When you get a good deal, it's a bargain.
At night, the horses are kept in the barn.
That's not small, it's large.
Rabbits like to munch on carrots.
We grow vegetables in our garden.
Another name for a rabbit is a hare.
It's not butter, it's margarine.
The bird on a pirate's shoulder is a parrot.

We Have
EVERYTHING®
on Anything!

With more than 19 million copies sold, the Everything® series has become one of America's favorite resources for solving problems, learning new skills, and organizing lives. Our brand is not only recognizable—it's also welcomed.

The series is a hand-in-hand partner for people who are ready to tackle new subjects—like you!

For more information on the Everything® series, please visit *www.adamsmedia.com*

The Everything® list spans a wide range of subjects, with more than 500 titles covering 25 different categories:

Business	History	Reference
Careers	Home Improvement	Religion
Children's Storybooks	Everything Kids	Self-Help
Computers	Languages	Sports & Fitness
Cooking	Music	Travel
Crafts and Hobbies	New Age	Wedding
Education/Schools	Parenting	Writing
Games and Puzzles	Personal Finance	
Health	Pets	